Soaring Past the Pain

The Resiliency to Triumph Over Past Traumatic Situations

Dedication

To Eula, Eddie, Aunt Nancy, and Mom, you all are my village. Thank you for raising me. I am so grateful for the role you played in my life. If it were not for your love and support, I would not be the person I am today. Regardless of the obstacles that attempted to stop me from becoming the best version of myself, I made it.

To my husband, Father, Brother, and children respectively, thank you for encouraging and supporting me through the writing process.

I love you all!

Special Acknowledgment

To Aunt Rosetta, thank you for being a mentor. I want to thank you for being who you are. You helped me by modeling me towards a drug-free lifestyle, being a mother to your children, and a supportive partner. You never judged me as I navigated through life, and I am so thankful to you.

Love Ayisha

Table of Content

Message to the reader

I am so excited that I get the opportunity to encourage and inspire you to soar above anything that is attempting to way you down, and I mean anything! Giving up is not an option. Growing up, I did not have the language to open up and share what I was going through. What happened in our home needed to remain in our house, but I have learned that you cannot heal what you do not confront.

When I became a middle school counselor, I realized that many children were still facing life-altering situations just as I did. The type of cases that graduate school did not prepare me for, but my life experiences did. I talked to many students, and I have to admit that they were brave and influential individuals that boldly told their truth. There are systems in place to help some children. However, the truth is that the state agencies that are in place will not be able to rescue children from all traumatic situations. I learned that as I walked through life — some people will have to go through circumstances that will shape them for the good and the bad. Because I have traveled this path before some people and after some people, the real question is how do I overcome the traumatic experiences and avoid repeating the cycle?

Introduction

As the tears roll down my chubby cheeks, and the thoughts rang through my head, repeatedly reminding me that I cannot do this anymore! I am leaving! Is this what life is all about? I have to do something about this because I cannot take it anymore. I had reachedmy breaking point! So many thoughts fluttered through my mind while I packed my sky blue bag with my clothes. Where can I go? How will I get there? My bag was packed and ready to go, and it was hidden in my closet. As the tears poured down my face, I thought, why me? That question went unanswered for years. I wanted to run away, but where would I go? Ugh, I hate this! Why won't she stop?

My brother and I shared a room, so he knew all about my plans to leave. I did not have any place to go. I was contemplating leaving with no place to go in order to save myself and the pain of leaving my brother behind. Then, there is my mother who needs me even if she doesn't realize it. God, help me! I never got mad at God, my hope remained anchored in Him. Why? I was always told that God was good, so He would surely give me a better life. Have you ever felt like the world was on your shoulders at a young age? I longed for a healthy childhood, a normal life, but my life continued...some good days and some days not so good.

Have you ever wondered why you were born? If you are or have been facing challenges after challenges in life, you may have asked this question many times. I hope that you have not thought of reasons to give up or leave life prematurely. You have more life in you to live. I had many reasons to give up, but what would that do, I would never see my future. I was a little girl with a lot of hope; I just wished that I could take some of the experiences away. In my heart, I knew that one day the pain would end.

I was taught that my inner voice is my conscience. However, as I continued to live and experience God, I would like to offer a different perspective. Children are on the mind of Christ. Christ was leading and guiding me through the hard times, obstacles, the horrific times, and the mountains of generational curses which attempted to suck me into the painful cycles of my family's past. Recently, I had a surgery called a hysterectomy. Prior to the surgery, the plan was to have a 3 to 4 weeks healing process, possibly going back to work in three weeks. When I woke up in the recovery room after the surgery, I felt pain in my lower abdomen, I knew that my healing process was going to be longer, and then, the nurse explained it to me. I was in so much pain! Excruciating pain! This pain was a pain that I had never felt before— I was passing out. I laid there and moved my head left and right. I looked at my husband, who was sitting at my right, and I could not talk to him.

After I woke up a couple of times and fell back asleep, I heard the voice of the Lord say, "Remember this pain." I would like to share with you that I could never forget the pain. After that moment, I begin to walk through a painful healing season physically and spiritually as the layers of my past unfolded. As each painful layer waspeeled back and the process started, I grieved for the child I am writing about— I grieved for me. God is incredible! He never begins a work in you without completing it. Little did I know that it was time to share my testimony in hopes to free those who are bound. I never knew that I was bound, I lived my life each day and never identified the layers of pain. When I reached the painful areas, the Holy Spirit began to comfort me through it, so that bitterness and anger did not arise. That was not the purpose of this book. This was not the purpose of rehashing the hurt. The Holy Spirit whispered, "You are writing from a healed place, an overcomer, everything that attempted to stop you is behind you." The purpose was to be able to articulate to the reader the steps of overcoming traumatic hurt. The same grace that was extended to me, God has offered to others. Often, our traumatic wounds could allow you to harden your heart against the Lord when He attempts to talk to you. If that is you, freedom is near. I pray that my testimony will allow you to soften your heart to the voice of the Lord in order to provoke healing.

As a part of the calling God has on my life, I get to speak life and positivity into the lives of broken people. I feel like this is my purpose and my calling. The more I talked to students who walked in my office with a heavy burden, I knew I was fulfilling my purpose, as they left recharged. I realized that there were some situations, traumatic situations that left and/or will leave a lifetime imprint of pain and regret. Young children go through difficult situations with the adults that are raising them. As a child, I carried the responsibility, and no one would ever know how much the heaviness weighed me down. In those moments, the word strong would come to my mind. I recognized that this is the "Strong" that I have been called all my life. Sometimes, I hated that word because I was just living on the good days, but trying to survive during the bad days. Somehow, the term "Strong" followed me throughout my life. Often, I did not feel strong, but people continued to refer to me as "Strong" whenever I shared pieces of my life's journey. Get ready as I tell you all about overcoming the traumatic situations that I thought I could not escape.

Chapter 1

Strength

The Strongest people are not those who show strength in front of us but those who win battles we know nothing about

Throughout my life, I was always called "Strong," and I could not understand why or what it meant. However, we had a huge secret that could have broken up our whole family. My mother, my brother, and I were like the three musketeers until "It" happened. "It" was the secret, the destroyer, the reason I wanted to leave and the reason I needed to stay because my family needed me. Sometimes, I just wanted to do something to make "It" go away, but I was just a kid. Sometimes, my brother and I would talk to our mom about "It," and she would cry and say, "I ask God to take the taste out of my mouth." During those conversations, my brother and I always felt like we did the right thing. Then other times, she would defend it and say, "I deserve to do it. I take care of y'all" this would leave us in fear and confusion. After experiencing that response many times, we would eventually back off because it hurt too much. It felt like she always chose "It" over us. It was an addiction to crack-cocaine, and I grew to hate it. Thankfully, my brother and I had each other to talk to because crack-cocaine affected our home weekly every payday or the payday of others who would come to our home to use it.

The trauma that I have experienced through many of the situations you will read about has left marks within and has shown up in the area of mistrust, rejection, anda muffled voice. For example, if someone lied to me, it would silently trigger suspicion. This is as a result of my relationship with my mother because of the broken promises to stop. A mental health trigger is an external event or circumstance that may produce very uncomfortable emotional or psychiatric symptoms, such as anxiety, panic, discouragement, despair, or negative self-talk. I called it a silent trigger because I was not aware of the root. My thoughts were, "I could never trust you, why are you hurting me? Or always digging into the situation." This is unhealthy, and it harbors unforgiveness, which turns into a burden called bitterness. The burdens are heavy. In certain circumstances, I have gone from zero to one hundred because of the thoughts resurfacing, but it has nothing to do with the current situation. In other conditions, I could filter out foolishness quickly. Now, let us look at a person that has not experienced trauma; their storage would be clear, empty, and able to deal with the issue, forgive more leisurely, and move on.

(2 Colossians 3:13) "Be tolerant of one another and forgive each other if anyone has a complaint against another. Just as the Lord has forgiven you, you also should forgive."

(10 Ephesians 4:26-27) "Be angry, yet do not sin." Do not let the sunset while you are still angry, and do not give the Devil an opportunity to work. "

(14 Ephesians 4:31) "Get rid of your bitterness, hot tempers, anger, loud quarreling, cursing, and hatred."

I can tell you that this is not the will of God for my life or yours *John 3:2* says, "Dear friend, I pray that you may enjoy good health and that all may go well with you, even as your soul is getting along well." I want to encourage you, "do not give up…finish your race!" You could be an adolescent or an adult, as you read my testimony be encouraged to become the best version of yourself. Allow me to show you how strong you are and that God's hand is on your life even when reality may not look like it. Are you up for the challenge?

Now, let us explore a little. Do you have an "It"? Your "It" could be several things such as; feeling unwanted, poverty, drug abuse, physical or sexual abuse, molestation, suicide, overall something that has negatively affected your life. Due to the "It," some people may experience fear, paralysis, settling, being unauthentic, or living below the standards that God has created you to.

If you are recalling a past situation, do not allow the emotions to take you back. Your past cannot hurt you, you are an overcomer! You cannot heal what you do not confront.

What is the name of your "It"? Has it stopped you from becoming the best version of yourself? Yes or No (circle)

If so, how has it stopped you? (Failing to thrive, loss of hope, etc.) When did you internally shut down? If you answered these questions, you have just confronted the "It." Take a deep breath and celebrate YOU!

Now, replace the negative words that have been spoken to you by family, friends, and yourself with the correct lyrics. Write a new song! I am talking about the negative words that you hear in your head, and no one knows that you are struggling with them (ex. You will never   be anything, you are stupid, you are just like your father or mother negatively, etc.). It is time to serve negativity an expiration notice.

Words of affirmations: "You are Brave. You are Bold. You are Courageous."

What I have learned is that many people have an "It factor." Therefore, you are not alone! What we will focus on is positivity, overcoming the barriers and obstacles, which the Bible calls the mountains you are facing. *Mark 11:23 "For truly I say to you, That whoever shall say to this mountain, Be you removed, and be you cast into the sea; and shall not doubt in his heart, but shall believe that those things which he said shall come to pass; he shall have whatever he said."* To finish the race of life, you have to adopt a positive mantra, song, and quote, something inspiring! It should speak to you, shake you and get you going— it should have the ability to move you when depression is setting in. It would be your reminder to slap you into a fighter's mode. My mantra was, "I will not become a statistic!" This reminds me of every negative word spoken about me, every cynical look, but I made a decision that I will never give up on me!

Chapter 2

Identity

My mother and father dated in their late teens, which led to a beautiful birth of their first daughter, they named her Ayisha. After becoming pregnant, my mother was excited about the pregnancy; however, she was in 12th grade, so of course, she was not ready. When my father found out that my mother was pregnant, he enlisted in the Army to provide for the family. Before this, he was a high school student, hanging with friends, smoking marijuana, and earning illegal money. My parents were married when I was 4 months old. We traveled to Hawaii, Kentucky, and Virginia as a military family. When I was 4 years old, my father received orders to report to Germany and my brother and I went with my mother back to New York. After we returned to New York, we later learned that moving back to New York was not the best environment for my mother. Familiar friends and places would eventually lead her down a path that could affect the entire family.

We moved in with our grandmother and uncle. My brother and I slept on the floor on a mattress in the living room in my grandmother's two-bedroom apartment. She was the sweetest person. She loved to dance, cook, and she was always the life of the party.   The only meal we did not like was liver. Man, my grandmother would check our plates to make sure that we ate enough food The days my grandmother cooked liver for dinner, my brother and I would sit at the table plotting how we were going to get rid of the liver before my grandmother made us sit   there longer. When I think back on it, it was funny, but at the time, it was not funny. Therefore, my brother and I would walk to my grandmother's room and show her our plate She would look at the plate, and she would say, "Eat some more"! We went back to the table, and we would try to spread the food out all over the plate to trick her, but she was on to us. My grandmother would do my hair— she had the task of straightening my hair, which meant taking the black iron hot comb and pulling it through my hair, even the hairs on the back of my neck. She would yell at me when I felt the heat on the back of my neck, "keep still, Eisha!" Often she burnt my ear and neck, and told me I should not have moved. I was so glad when I got a perm.

A great summer day looked like summer camp with project pride, going to free lunch, and buying ice cream from Mr. Softy, the ice cream truck, buying a slice of pizza for one dollar, and hanging out with my friends cheering on the block. The older folks would sit on the benches that were in front of the building, and sometimes my grandmother would watch us from the upstairs window. Whenever the ice cream truck came, we would talk or yell, "Granny, we need money to buy an ice cream" She would throw down the money by wrapping up the coins in the middle of the dollars. I miss those days! The older I got, we had cheer practice, and we would battle girls from other blocks, this always brought a crowd in! I never felt shy when I cheered, I was very free to be me, and I loved it. We would jump rope, straight rope and double dutch, we played red light, green light, and red rover, and kick the can. We had great times, but sometimes some of the dark days overshadowed life itself.

One day, my mom did not come home, and another day passed, and another day, no mom. This is the day I realized that my mother had a problem. My grandmother was worried about her, and she was talking on the phone, so I did what any average child would do. I eased dropped. My mom had not been home in a couple of days, and my grandmother was mad and scared. Guess what, I was scared too because I noticed that my mom has not come home. Then she found her at one of her friend's houses hiding in a closet, and she had to put her into rehab for 10- days. My grandmother had no idea that I was listening to her conversations. Therefore, my grandmother told my brother and me that she was in the hospital for 10- days and we could not touch her, but we could go see her. My granny, brother, and I caught the bus and walked until we got in front of a building. My mom waved at us by sticking her hand out of the window. That is it! We walked towards the bus stop, and I remembered thinking, "That is it" repeatedly. Do you know how I felt? Confused and empty, but by the look on my grandmother's face, I knew that it was not the time to ask questions. I was happy to see her from afar and knowing that she was okay. We never talked to anyone about it, not even to each other— this was our secret.

As I searched my family, on both my mother and my father's side, there are many negative generational cycles. Drug addiction was in my father's family, as well. Do you see a pattern? "A generational curse is believed to be passed down from one generation to another due to rebellion against God. If your family line has displayed divorce, incest, poverty, anger, addictions, rebellion or other ungodly patterns, you are likely to encounter temptation in those areas. It is the enemy's plan to hook you and interrupt your life in such a way that you believe the illusion of what you see. I personally never accepted that I would use drugs even though it was all around me. I always had a great level of hope in my heart, but what I did identify with is the facts. If drugs had my mother and grandmother, it would not have me. This was an inner vow I made before I knew what an inner vow is. An inner vow is a determination set by the mind and heart into all the being in early life. Therefore, the chances would increase that I could struggle with the generational curse of addiction. I was adamant that I would never develop a drug addiction. I have seen the effects up close and personal, and that was enough for me.

Many people assumed that I would be a product of my environment, but my mindset never allowed me to accept that. The Bible says that these curses are tied to choices." *Deuteronomy 30:19 says "we can either choose life and blessing or death and cursing."*   I have always been a person that is willing to learn from someone else's mistakes. I never looked down on my mother's addiction. For years, I thought she chose drugs over my brother and me. Therefore, I hate drugs, and it is my hatred for drugs that kept me from trying it. If I could fight crack I would have. It is okay to laugh now, but this hurt as a child. My brother and I felt like we could not win against it — I could never accept it as part of the family. Addiction is the fact or condition of being addicted to a particular thing, substance, or activity. When I was in college, I took an addictions class, and I had an excellent instructor, Mr. Dennis. He did not know my background, but he painted good examples of a person on crack and what they would do to get high. When he gave examples of how an addict would drop to the floor to find the crack, I wanted to sink in my seat. I also wanted to fight it because I felt like it won. Overall, the class was tough but informative, and I quickly knew that I would not go into addictions counseling.

What does a normal childhood look like? Is it a two-parent household, a single-parent home, or living with family members? I often wondered if what I was experiencing was normal. As a child, I did not realize the projects meant poverty it was my norm. Today, I can see and understand a lot more. After facing adversity, I could choose to be angry with my mother. Generally, when someone is mad because they have endured pain, hurt, rejection, etc., it actually feels good to have a person to reflect on their disappointment. I could point the finger at my father because he was not there. Do I have the right to hold this over them? Would that take away the hurt and disappointment? This is what many people fall prey to— finger- pointing the blame. I will admit that my mindset has always been optimistic. Whenever my back is against the wall, I come out swinging; fighting through the pain. Now, what I see is that my mother had fun as a teenager and tried drugs, and she became addicted. She did not know that she was going to become addicted because she would not have done it. Who would? My mother loved me and I loved her— I just did not accept the addiction. I wanted my mother to be free! Here is where I see the hand of the enemy; he robbed my mom because he is the author of addictions. My father was also fighting the same invisible enemy. My father was lured away and enticed by women; this is a trick of the enemy. My father fell prey and decided to act on specific circumstances, not realizing that the enemy had a plan so that he could never live the life he wanted to— this was a rough beginning. When you have two children involved, but it is a fight that families are still fighting today. Blaming others is a huge distraction. It is an invisible quicksand, once you are stuck in it; you sink, become submerged, and suffocate, and never reaching your full potential. To have the love and support of my parents mean the world to me, and the fact that the two of them were not perfect lets me know that I will never be perfect. I have been far from perfect trying to figure out life. I have intended to make the best decisions, but I fall short many times. This is why forgiveness is essential! If you continuously blame family and friends for the things that you may have experienced in life, you are in prison to the situational bondage. Accept the lifeline of and choose to forgive, you will be able to see the truth, the imperfections, the disappointments, the shame, and the failed attempts of your family members as they try to love you the best they could without having all of the tools. Forgiveness is a choice, but it is the key to unlock your clear path to freedom.

Affirmation: "You are a Conqueror! You are loved!"

Chapter 3

Who Am I

Did life shape me to be the person I am? I wish there was a manual for life. Was I supposed to have the heart to help others? My parents never reconciled after their separation. My mother never encouraged my brother or me to hate my father due to his absence. She allowed us to make our own decision. She had many family pictures of us in Hawaii, Kentucky, and Virginia. The images were loaded with laughter and good times. I can recall wishing that he would come and save us, but it never happened. I would always think about what life would be like if we were with him in Germany and Washington as a family. Sadly, I still had to adjust my dream in order to face reality. My grandfather became the father figure in my life. He would talk a lot to my brother and me about life. He spoke to me about drugs and told me to never use it. He explained the dangers of it, as I got older, I realized how much it hurt my grandfather that his children used drugs, so he spent a lot of time convincing or trying to save my brother and I. I appreciated every word that he said to us. In these moments, I felt good because I witnessed many situations with drugs, and he was the only one that talked to me about it. He was wealthy, had a great job, and lived in a better neighborhood. He would pick us up in his Cadillac and talk the entire way to his home. When we visited him, he gave us a glimpse of what healthy middle-class life looked like. I would always compare the difference I would experience being at his home versus being in the projects. Co-op city buildings were safe, a tenant had to buzz you in, and it was clean with absolutely no urine in the elevators. In the projects, the elevators smelled like urine, anyone could come in the building, and I had to watch my back all the time. My grandfather lived for many years, and when sickness began, eventually he passed away. When my grandfather died, I heard the voice of the Lord say "Now you will have a relationship with your dad."

Every failed marriage has three sides to the story. There is my mom's side, my dad's side, and the truth. What I have learned and accepted is that their breakup has nothing to do with me. I wondered if my dad were here throughout my life; would he have been able to stop some of the situations that went on. The truth is, I will never know! I know that the enemy does not like marriage, and his job is to tear down marriages. Every wedding starts with the intent of being successful, after all, who wants to marry to fail. When my father and I reconciled and began to have conversations, I told him that he did not have to leave my brother and me if he left my mom. This was a thought that would travel through my mind so many times throughout my life, so when I delivered this word to him, I did not know how he was going to take it, but I was standing in my truth.

Thankfully, he was man enough to stand in his pain, which helped our relationship flourish.

The void of not having a parent, a father to a little girl, left a deep void, a hole filled with darkness in my heart. The reconciliation of a daughter and father relationship would take some work from both of us. Gratefully, we were up for the challenge— I can recall saying "Dad and I felt nothing." All my life, I have been saying, "Mom," and regardless of the difficulties that we have gone through in life, and I felt love, family, and belonging. However, when I went to say, dad, I felt nothing, so I started calling my dad "Pops." My dad would often begin conversations telling me how much he loved me, and when I was born, he knew that I was an angel when he looked into my eyes. I will be honest; it was difficult at first. When he called me a baby girl because, in my mind, I was   thinking if it meant anything to you, you would have stayed. Sometimes in life, we have to push past the voided areas that are within our hearts. God is all about reconciliation, and if you have ever gone through unforeseen situations that were meant to tear your family apart, I have learned that God has the key to healing.

One day, my father and I had a conversation, and he was puzzled as to how we will move forward and with my counselor hat on, I said we need to make new memories. I wholeheartedly believe this! Little did I know that it would take a lot of pressing on my behalf. What I learned is walking out reconciliation with my father looked like staying focused on the new memories. It also meant not allowing the negative words that I may have heard throughout my life to resurface, while we were in our rebuilding stage. When the negative thoughts arose to the point that I could not shake, I learned to talk to him about it, answering every question, or adding a comforting word. I remember telling him about the situations that went on in my life because I knew that he probably wanted to know but just did not know how to ask. When he said, I am sorry that you went through all of those things, and I wish I were there to take it all away, something snapped in my heart. It was like if there was a crook in the line that had snapped back into place, and the essence of peace came over me. I have never felt anything like that before. To be honest, I did not know that I needed that response. I learned to live life according to the cards I was dealt. I could not cry over not having a father my entire life, right? God had a plan to bring healing and restoration, and I moved into a place of instant forgiveness.

Now, that my heart was able to accept the words of love that my dad was able to speak into my life, he began to talk to me about the little girl I was. He described me as the helper, nurturing, an Angel, friendly, bold, confident, and always communicating with others. As I watched him express me, a thought ran through my mind, what happened to my voice? Here I got a download from God, sometimes I thought the person that I have become loving nurturing wanting to help came from helping my mom, but in these conversations with my father, I realize that

Jeremiah 1:5 was displaying in my life. *"Before I formed you in the womb, I knew you;   before you were born, I sanctified you; I ordained you a prophet to the nations."* What I saw is that the enemy launched attacks against me at a young age to strip me of my voice. Look around in your life if you have been under attack since a young child, chances are God has placed a gift in you for the world. It is the enemy's job to make sure that you do not become the person that God has ordained you to become. However, Yahweh is a present help, and He never leaves or forsakes His children.

I speak to you now from a place of healing to look back over my life, the rocky beginnings had nothing to do with my mom or my dad and has everything to do with my gift. It is the enemy's job to have you pointing the fingers at whomever you feel may have wronged you. This is why forgiveness is the first step. Nobody sets out in life to have something strangle the life out of you such as drug addictions, alcohol addictions, pornography, physical, sexual, and emotional abuse, but the truth of the matter is that when you're facing situations like these, which can suck the life out of you and all those around you— there is strength and pricing through any situation you're facing. If I was not resilient or able to bounce back, that would mean that the enemy won. This is not the plan of God for your life! Hear me right; it is God's will that you live an abundant life, that you flourish, that your families are saved, that your generations are changed, and we all return to Him. If you have allowed situations to paralyze you or to immobilize you, I call you right now to come out of that place, I urge you to stand up. If you are still breathing and you are reading this book, God is giving you the authority to walk out of every situation that has attempted to take your life under. He has called you to be resilient, He has called you to bounce back, and you can do it, for He is with you.

Dear God,

I thank you for never leaving or forsaking me. I thank you for being there and for blocking the things that are seen and unseen. Take the hurt and the pain away from my heart. I do not want it anymore. I invite you to come in and fill my heart with joy, love and laughter because I deserve it because. I know this is your plan for my life and I am ready to receive all that you are willing to give me Lord. Comfort me in those moments where there is no one there for me. I accept your hugs, I accept your love, I am pulling down the walls, and I will let you in God. I trust you, God, I am ready to rebuild my life, and see you take the wheel. You are more significant than the situation that I have faced God. I give you authority over everything that has come into my life, which has been birthed into my heart and my mind, and I say God I don't want it anymore I surrender to you, Lord God, I am excited to walk with you for the rest of the days of my life. God show me who you intended for me to be before situations came about to change the person that I was supposed to be. God, I am willing to do the work. I accept you, I accept your help, I want your help, I agree with your love even if I don't know what love looks like God you allow your Holy Spirit to teach me what love looks like God. In Jesus' name, Amen.

Little did I know that the missing puzzle pieces to my life would be added by my father. I am so grateful for walking through the process. I cannot tell you that it was an easy process because it was not, but as you walk through your journey, know that I am praying with you and thanking God for your healing.

Chapter 4

Adversity

You can't Be Brave if you've only had wonderful things happen to you. –Mary Tyler Moore

My mom found her first apartment located at Webster Avenue. It was not too far from my grandmother's apartment; we could walk there. We did a lot of walking in New York. We had a two-bedroom apartment. My mom had a room, and my brother and I shared a room. My brother was five, and I was seven years old at the time. At some point, my mom would have friends over; these people never visited my grandmother's home. One night, my brother and I were sleeping in my mother's room, and I was awakened by my mother calling my name. When I got up, what I saw was horrifying, but at the time, my focus was on helping my mom. I am a natural fighter or just stupid. I walked out of the bedroom and into the living room, and I saw a man strangling my mother. His hands were around her neck, and her eyes were popping out of her head. Her legs had already kicked the living room table, so her feet were kicking the air. I made my way past them and ran into the kitchen, grabbed a knife, and stood behind the man and yelled, "Get off my mother!" The man jumped up, looked at me, and ran out of the door! He ran past me, I did not flinch, I was bold! My mother grabbed me and hugged me so tight while she sobbed. I hugged her back, and she cried and cried. I put the knife down, and we never talked about how it made me feel. We talked about why the man was strangling her, and the reason why is because all the drugs were gone, and someone was supposed to bring more but never came back. As I aged and looked back on this situation, what bothered me the most is that there is no way that the man was afraid of a little girl with a knife, probably a butter knife.

In my heart, I knew that God was there. Did he see my guardian angels that are taller and bigger than a little seven-year-old? I believe that the Spirit of God commanded me to speak to the evil spirit, and it ran. When I gave my life to Christ in 2002, I was 25 years old. It was the day after my birthday. After attending service for a few months, I went up to the altar for prayer and knelt with a heavy heart. In those moments of talking to the Lord, He began to show me all of the incidents that you will read about. I wept, but I knew that He was always there; I felt that I was having the ultimate experience because He wanted me to see that He did not cause those situations, and I felt the comfort and realized that His hand is all over me always. My alter experience was humbling; yet comforting. It was as if I found my way back after a long journey.

(Jeremiah 1:5) "Before I formed you in the womb, I knew you before you were born, I set you apart; I appointed you as a prophet to the nations."

One day after the incident, my mom and her boyfriend, Mr. Jeffrey, came to get me out of the house and said, "Ayisha come quick." Therefore, I got up and quickly ran with her. We ran out of the door and up the steps to the pavement and down the street. I remembered trying to keep up as I was thinking about what was going on. When we reached Mr. Jeffrey, he had a man detained. They wanted me to identify the man that was choking her. My mind began to race. What if I pointed out the wrong person? I was so scared that I was not sure, but I told him that he was the person. It was an impromptu lineup New York style. What is New York-style? My mom was from the streets, so her way of defending was all that she knew when I said yes that is him. Mr. Jeffery beat him up on the sidewalk in front of me and everyone that walked by. I cannot tell you what ran through my mind. In the streets, that is revenge or karma. As I got older from time to time, I would wonder if he was the right person, everything happened so quickly!

My mom had a friend that would visit, and then he began to spend nights. He would help clean up, and my brother and I knew him as being a body in the home. We did not have a relationship, and he never felt like a family to us. He would be in the room with my mother getting high, so I never trusted him. One day, I was outside playing, and I needed to use the restroom, so I went into the basement, where our apartment was located. This day was different— as I approached the door, I was just aware of everything. Therefore, I walked into the apartment, and I immediately saw that he was different, his eyes were red, and he was looking at me weird. It was so creepy that I could not use the restroom. I immediately avoided direct contact with him and went into the bathroom.

As I closed the door, I could feel his presence waiting for me to open the door. I stood there and had an open vision, and it was a plan of escape. I got instructions as to what I needed to do, I opened the door, and he was waiting for me. In my vision, I saw that I needed to run left and run through the door, which would be open for me, do not look back and run through all three doors until I ran up the stairs to get help. When I stepped out of the door Mr. Thomas approached, he asked me if he could see my breast, I yelled, "No" and took off. Here was another God moment! I did what I saw in the open vision. I was so afraid— I went to my mother's friend's apartment and waited for her. Mrs. Annette went and got my brother and kept us with her until my mom came. When my mother came, she was upset. Mr. Thomas had left before we got there.

Sometimes, the pain and hurt of a traumatic experience can be so overwhelming that it overshadows God's soft voice. You do not have to go to church to have a God moment. God loves and adores you and will show up regardless of if you have a relationship with Him or not. That is grace and mercy. *Jeremiah 6:14* New International Version (NIV) "They dress the wound of my people as though it were not serious. 'Peace, peace,' they say,   when there is no peace."

If you are recalling a situation, write your God moment below.

____

____

____

____

____

____

Sometime after the situation, my mom's boyfriend, Mr. Jeffrey, saw Mr. Thomas walking downtown and guess what? He fought him in the streets for what he attempted to do to me. Now that I am an adult, I know that fist fighting is not the best way to solve situations. It may feel right at the time, but it does not heal the inward scars. Growing up in the streets, you learn to fight. You have to fight for your respect. You fight if someone poses as a threat to you or your family; you need to be ready to defend yourself. My mother instilled this into my brother and me. As I got older, I realized that you can go to jail for putting your hands on people and I've adopted a mindset shift. I learned that I had to fight with my mind— that was the best way to win.

Whew, that was a lot! As I recall some of the events from my childhood, it is not easy. It hurts, and I have grieved for the little girl. I realized that I was so busy trying to be whoever my mom needed me to be that I never uttered how I felt. It was not fair and created layers which have led me towards writing this book. Things happened, and we dealt with it at the time and moved on. It is amazing how we go through traumatic situations, but yet we move on as if what just happened did not affect us. I believe we are in a time where we need to realize how some situations have changed us. Some people may need to speak to a mental health counselor. I know that so many people in my culture do not believe in counseling, and it is disheartening because there is fantastic help available to those in need. Let me help you out, seeing a counselor does not mean that you are mentally ill, crazy, or need medication. For example, if you have been told that you are dumb every day from the age of 7 to the age of 25, which is a total of 6,570 times you have heard it. At some point, you will have adopted this negative word, questioned yourself when you fail at something, or are likely to mentally war against it. Now, imagine dealing with traumatic issues such as molestation, physical and emotional abuse, abandonment, bullying, rape, drugs, etc. these situations do not define you. Seeking counseling will allow you to walk through some tight areas with support and gain clarity to help you continue to run your race in life. There are so many wounded people walking around hurt because people are afraid to face the situations. If it is in the past, you've already passed it. You get to decide if you will allow it to keep you held captive. Let it go by pushing past all uncertainness, you owe yourself a great fight. I am cheering for you!

Do not allow past situations to hinder your future.

Affirmation: "Empowerment "You are Resilient! You are Confident.""

Steps to Freedom

Here are some steps to freedom that you can use whether your situation is current or in the past. Applying these steps led me to freedom.

Steps	You Will Triumph	You Will Remain the Same
Step I. Forgiveness This is hard! This is important!	This step is for you and not the person or the situation that has you burdened. When you forgive the person, this will allow your heart to feel lighter.	Your heart hardens, and you become a prisoner to the situation. You may drink or use drugs to help you forget or become numb.

Step II. Confront it	You must face the situation face to face. Determine in your mind that you will not allow the situation to have the final say.	Ignore it. Act like it did not happen.
Step III. Accept it	It happened. It does not define who you are. Take what you had learned and push forward.	Unable to because your heart is hardened.
Step IV. Overcome	Go through the purification process. Impurities are removed. Become authentic.	Unable to be your authentic self. Impurities remain within and is used as weighs and sin.
Step V. Celebrate	You've done hard work! You can feel the freedom! You	You will celebrate some areas in your life, but you will

	have trusted the process!	never celebrate the person you indeed are without freeing yourself.

Chapter 5

Back to the Safety Hub

Psalm 127:3 "Children are a heritage from the Lord, offspring a reward form Him."

In my third grade year, we moved back to my grandmother's house. My mother said, "She knew it was time to leave the area!" She always had a way to know her limits, when enough is enough— she would ever act on it. While we were living back at my grandmother's apartment, my brother and I did not have a room of our own, so we slept on a mattress in the living room. When I look back over my life, I hate that we were always on the floor because it represented a low place. Over the years, I adopted a mantra from sleeping on the floor; the only place I can go from here is up! So, when we lived at my grandmother's apartment with her, my mom, uncle, brother, and sometimes my grandmother's boyfriend. During this time, my mother continued to struggle with her addiction. The good thing was that we had my grandmother home with us when my mother was out working or hanging out. My mother would spend time with us going to the movies, playing cards, and shopping on 3rd avenue. With my grandmother's support, my mother was able to enroll in cosmetology school, work, make time for us, and socialize. Times were not always stressful, but I have to admit the traumatic situations did leave an impact-full weight on my shoulders. During the time of living with my grandmother, I realized that my uncle had an addiction problem as well. My uncle was very cool, except at night, when he would pace back and forth to the door with

paranoia after using drugs. I have learned from watching my family members struggle with drugs because it has a different effect on everyone. What I have experienced is that for them to get the "High" they seek, some people will steal, lie, and simply show a lack of respect for the others that are around them. At that time in my life, I took it personally because I did not understand. In the 1980s, the crack epidemic was terrible, and it left widespread addictions, deaths, and drug-related crimes.

One year, my grandfather took my brother and me back to school shopping on Delancey Street in New York. This was the first and last time that he did this and my mom was surprised, I remember her talking about it. I always felt safe with my grandfather. I would have loved to live with him, but he would not rescue my mother and bring her drug addiction into his home. More than likely, she would not have taken up his offer because he had rules and boundaries. So, we were so excited, we went shopping and brought us two outfits. Another one of my uncles came to visit one night, and he decided to steal our school clothes. The clothes that my grandfather bought; maybe that is why he never took us shopping again. My brother and I had our first day of school outfit laying out on the couch. When I woke up with full excitement to grab our clothes and get ready for the first day of school, I walked to the sofa, and there were no clothes. Immediately we scream, "Mama, where are my clothes," my mother says it is on the couch; we told her no mom it is not there. When she came in to look for it herself, she said, it's gone! She began to look in the closet where the other clothes were hanging, and the two outfits that we had worn were still there. She realized that one of her coats was gone and then she said, "Carl must have taken it." I want to paint this picture for you out of the two outfits, the one I love the most was the one that was on the couch, so I was heartbroken. My uncle was going to jail for five years. Later in life, he admitted to stealing our clothes. He expressed he did not care because he was going to jail. When we got together as a family, we talked about this, and we laughed about it now. I forgave him because he accepted responsibility for everything that he did. Being able to forgive is essential! Forgiveness is not something we do for other people; we do it for ourselves so that we can move on. The reality is that it is easier to forgive when someone admits they have done wrong to you.

On the other hand, my other uncle that lived with us would steal from us too. We would hide our money in our shoes, as below the sole of the shoe, and try to put the shoe in a different place, and for some reason, he would always find our hiding spot. Sometimes, he would just take my money, and my brother would share his wealth with me when we would go to the candy store after school. My brother and I were so close that we slept on the same mattress, we shared each other's money, and we kept our secrets. As the older child, I kept secrets from my brother about my mom that I felt he was too young to know about.

Sometimes, I would go on a field trip through my uncle's room before my grandmother would clean it. I probably should not have done it, but his behavior was different from my mother's, and I was curious. My grandmother told us not to go in there, and she would keep the door closed. What is in the room? My grandmother always went in and cleaned the place up, but sometimes I would get in there before her and see the white powder which was baking soda on the floor, a spoon that was burnt, empty crack bottle tops with different colors all over the place. When I was in his room, I would see the tools that he used to cook crack cocaine. I remember seeing the crack bottles were also all around outside. New York had a massive drug problem, and as a kid, I was aware of it because of the commercials to prevent drug use, and from my encounters in my home.

In my late thirties, my brother and I wanted to talk with my uncle about our childhood experience. This turned out to be an epic failure. My thoughts were maybe this would be great to air it, and talk about how it affected our life at the time. It turned into a huge argument! First, he denied it, then his exact words were, "Oh, you're talking about something that happened over

30 years ago." Our intent was not understood at all, I was misunderstood a lot in life. After realizing that he would not be able to own his truth, we had to forgive him, and so we did. Deep down in my heart, I knew that the addiction had brought the behaviors out of him, but it would have been kind to apologize— I have learned that in life, you will not always get the apology that you deserve. Therefore, I had to forgive him for myself, and so I prayed for him. In life, I have learned that forgiveness is for you even though you feel like you are letting someone off the hook.

My grandmother was a Certified Nursing Assistant, and sometimes she would take my brother and I to work with her. On the weekend, Mr. Fernell would watch us. Mr. Fernell enjoyed drinking vodka, he would drink out of little short glasses straight vodka, and he drank water behind it. He would make breakfast for my brother and me, and we hated it because the eggs would be loose or runny. One day, my brother and I were at home, and Mr. Fernell was the only adult at home. I went into my grandmother's room, and he was sitting on the bed. The way her room was designed as soon as you walked into it, there was the bed. That's where he sat. There was a nightstand, and he would always have a drink there. I do not know why I went into the room that day, but I know he looked at me, grabbed me, and said, "Let me teach you how to kiss. Because he grabbed me and pulled me between his legs, it was difficult to get away, but as his tongue was in my mouth, I continued to push him off me, he let go, and I ran. I did not tell my mother until I was 30, and I never told my grandmother because I knew she would not believe me. I had to protect myself; I was instructed to always be in the room with my brother present, so everywhere he went in the house, I went, "Another God moment," because there is no way that an eight-year-old could think like this on her own. When Mr. Fernell grabbed me, there were only two of us in the room, I do not believe that he would have done that— had there been someone else in there. So, any time my brother left out of the room, I would too; it did not matter if I wanted to stay. When these instructions came to me, I never forgot them. My brother would play with his wrestling man, and I would play with my Barbie in the same room. Boys are different, sometimes they switch up and move around, and so everywhere he went, I would go. In my heart, I believe it protected me from Mr. Fernell. He never tried to kiss me again, I never made eye contact with him unless other people were in the room, and I did not look at him very long.

One night, Mr. Fernell had way too much to drink. My brother, and I were sitting in the living room. My grandmother was sitting at the dining room table with her back turned to the kitchen, and Mr. Fernell was in the kitchen. I do not know what she said to make him angry, but he pulled back her chair and she fell to the floor. I remember getting close to my brother. We sat on the couch and watched. He had her in front of us, on all fours in the living room. She was crying hard, yelling for him to stop, and yelling for me to go and get help. When I looked at the situation to get to the door to get the support we needed, I would have had to run around in the kitchen to run around and run past them. His eyes were red, and he looked at me and said as he held a big knife in his hand, "If she runs to the door, I will slit her throat" I recognize the evil spirit in him, and I knew that he was serious. My grandmother continued to cry, telling me to go, but in that moment of looking at him and he had the knife, I knew that he would have harmed me, so I sat there with my brother until he was done with my grandmother. He did not stab her, but he physically abused her. After the situation, he was still present, not entirely gone out of her life, but he did not stay at the house as much. We never talked about it, and I wondered if she was mad because I did not listen.

Whew! That is a lot! Let us take a moment and reflect; chances are that if you have gone through anything in your life, and it began to come to the surface that is looking for your God moment. Did you get angry with themand shut him out?

If you are saying I did not have a God moment, I have good news for you. This is that moment. Here is my prayer for you:

Dear God,

I want to thank you for allowing the reader to read my testimony. I thank you right now, that he or she is experiencing their God moment. You are a healer, and You can fill the void that was caused by a painful situation. God I give you

____________ (the situation) I release it! It is too much for me to carry. I have been carrying it for too long, and I want to be free. Right now, I accept Jesus Christ as my savior and Lord over every traumatic situation. (Breathe) Uproot every negative word that was spoken over my life. I renounce coming into agreement with every negative word. I deserve a better life. I believe in me. I love me. You love me, and I receive Your love. In Jesus' name, Amen.

Chapter 6

Enough is Enough

We always believed in God, but we did not attend church regularly. We went on New Year's Eve and Easter Sunday. We said our prayers at night and blessed our food. I would have dreams, but I never talked about them. Dreams are a gift from God. One day, my relatives from Brooklyn came over and prayed over my brother and me. Both of us were sitting on the couch, when my aunt began to pray for me, she put her hand over my head and prayed. I do not remember what she said as she prayed. My head was moving all over following her hand motion, and I just looked at my brother. She did the same thing to my brother. We just looked at each other because we had no idea what was going on. Then, they prayed over my mother and had her in a circle, and she was jumping and crying.

After this, my mom said, "We were going on a trip down south to visit our family, and my aunt lived behind Burger King." We were not super happy about Burger King, but we loved our mom, so we said, okay! We would be back right before ~~we went to~~ school after Labor Day. Then, we came to South Carolina, and after two days, my mom told us she found a job, and we were staying down here. I sobbed and cried and cried, she tricked us!

Our summer vacation had ended because South Carolina starts school earlier than New York. Man, this was the worst thing for us at that time, but it turned out to be the best thing for my mom.

We lived with my grand aunt Nancy who was the sweetest, loving person ever and a great cook. My aunt would open up her home to anyone. So now, I gained the temporary privilege of living in a middle-class neighborhood, a two-bedroom house with a yard, and a safe environment with great friends. I know you heard me say it was a two-bedroom house, so you are probably wondering where the three of us slept. We made a paddle on the floor in the living room, and that is where we slept. As I got older, my mind would always recall sleeping on the floor. I understand that we were in desperate times and that we lived with someone and that it was a temporary situation, however, at some point in my life, I hated the fact that I was on the floor for a lot of my life— it symbolized the bottom.

Sometimes, when you are in a rock-bottom situation, you have to look around and realize that there is no place you could go except up. This was encouraging to myself. This gave me permission to dream of a better life and seek after it.

My aunt worked at Park Circle elementary and guess what; that was the elementary school we attended. I was in the 5th grade, and my brother was in the 3rd grade. Therefore, each day I was able to see my Aunt Nancy serving lunch in the cafeteria.

Attending school at Park Circle elementary was not too bad. I made friends and my mom volunteered for field trips. The kids in my class loved her. My mother is always the life of the party, even if it is just a field trip. When we would have things in class, the students would always say, Ayisha, see if your mom can come. Life was short-lived at Park Circle elementary when my mom saved enough money, we moved into our apartment.

When we moved, my mom enrolled me in Chicora Elementary school in Charleston, South Carolina. My teacher's name was Mr. Graham, and what I learned in his class is that he had the right to paddle students. If you have never experienced watching someone get a paddle in the classroom, it is hilarious. As in any fifth-grade class, some students are just comedians, and of course, they're always boys. Mr. Graham nicknamed one of the boys in the class "Tough butt Victor," because he received a paddle frequently. So an episode of paddling in Mr. Graham's classroom would result in a disruption as Mr. Graham is teaching. Then, Mr. Graham would have to stop teaching to figure out which student had done something to the other student, and then, the excitement would happen. Girls would be paddled as well, but the boys would try to run, which made it more exciting. Mr. Graham had two paddles; one was thin for the girls, first-time paddles, or lite offenses. The other was thick with a lot of tape on the area that hits you, but this is the one he used for the boys. Once Mr. Graham figured out what happened, Mr. Graham would call the boy or student up to the front of the classroom and tell them to put their hands on the desk. Next, he would ask them to bend over and put their hands on the desk, and he would take the paddle, get to a position, and whack him on the butt, bam! The entire class would watch; it was as if someone was about to fight. Depending on how bad the situation was, some students got two whacks.

One day, I experienced the paddle, I was in the restroom with the other girls. The girls were making too much noise; I do not remember being a part of the sound because I was always quiet. Because of the loud noise, Mr. Graham was in the hallway waiting with the skinny paddle. When I came out of the door, I heard Mr. Graham yelled, "Line up," and as the girls went down the hall to go into the classroom, he whacked each one of them. I think I was the last one he looked at, and said you too and he whacked me. My mother would work and do the best she could to provide for us. She worked in housekeeping in the hospital or hotels. We did chores and tried not to make things harder for my mom. My brother and I became her support system.

Now that it was just the three of us. We were excited about a new beginning. We had gotten familiar with our new home in the low-income area. If you have ever had to deal with adversity, you learn to make the best of any situation. Do not allow your situation to overtake you, and if you are strong, you are always thinking and paying attention to the things that others may not realize. If you are the "Strong one," you are careful, cautious by nature, and you do not know why or maybe you do? You provide hope and joy to your family just by your presence.

If you do not know it, I am here to tell you! This transition brought on a different type of exposure called domestic violence. I knew about fighting because I was taught self-defense at an early age.

My aunt, friends, and mother taught me. My mother's words were, "If anyone hits your brother, you better jump in." This is a secret code in the same system that is taken if someone attempts to harm anyone in my family.

My mom would date, and the boyfriend would have the same addiction. Later on, in life, my mom shared with me that when men use drugs, it brings out an angry side of them. Sometimes, my brother and I would be watching television just minding our own business, and we would hear a thump or two thumps, and we would jump up and run to my mom's room door. As the oldest, I would go ballistic banging on the door, trying to get to my mother to make sure she was okay. Somewhere in seeing my mother struggle, the roles of responsibility would change. No, I did not work a full-time job, and I did not pay the bills; she did all that. However, I felt that I had to make sure she was okay, so I would always be protective of her. My mother did not like it when we would come to help her fight, she would come to the door and tell us to go back into our room. That left me feeling confused, defenseless, and empty. Afterward, we would talk about it; she would confirm that she was okay. Smiles, hugs, dinner and a movie would settle things back down. My thoughts were never expressed about how it made me feel that she did not want me to help her, but she taught me to defend my brother.

Now that I am an adult, I know that I had no business trying to fight a grown man and she was trying to protect us. We dwelled in the area for close to two years, moving three times, then we moved into a housing development called North Park Village.

When we lived in North Park Village, we had a two-bedroom townhome, my brother and I shared a room. This environment provided financial stability for our family. If she ever lost her job, we would still have a home that was a win for us because we would not have to go live with anyone again and sleep on the floor. While moving, my mom began to lean on me a little more. She taught me how to hold the bill money, and regardless of how much she begged me for the money, do not give it back to her. Therefore, I obeyed. When I look back, I realize how, when we lived with the other people, it helped me remain a child. Eventually, I began to hate the weekends or payday because those were the times that some of my mom's friends would come over to get high. Whenever the room door was shut, my brother and I knew it was going on. People would come up and down the stairs, and we would be sitting on the couch watching television. I remember observing as everyone would go in the room normal, and when they came out, they were different. She would come and check, and apparently, the television was too loud whenever she went out of the room because she would always turn it down— that was still the first indicator that she was getting high.

I wish I knew how to pray or words of power. All I could do was promise myself that I was going to college and getting away from here.

On payday, my mom would give me the bill money, and she explained to me that the phone bill, electric bill, or whatever bill needed to be paid. She gave me the money and emphasized, it does not matter what she says to me, I am not to give her the money. Whatever she says, do not give her the money! Since we had moved a couple of times before moving onto North Park Village, of course, I could comprehend that if we did not pay the bills, we would have to move or something would be turned off. Therefore, I took her seriously, and I knew that I had to help her. Therefore, this is about the eighth grade, and I was 13- years old. Some nights, I was able to tell her no, and she would leave me alone, but it felt like it took 20- times of saying it. Other nights she would get angry and in those moments was when I would give her the money. Those are the moments, I felt like a failure! She explained how important it was that I did not give her the money, so my family was counting on me when she gave me the money. I was the kind of kid that is a rule follower. However, as I watched her go through the addiction, I witnessed what it did to her on bad days. I challenged myself to find ways to outsmart her. I learned to hide the money under the pillow, and sometimes I woke up and it was still there, and other times it was gone— I had to fight for my family. I remember running out of places to hide the money, so I eventually hid the money in my panties. She never went in there! These events finally made me feel as though I wanted to give up, I wanted to go. I am tired, and I want out of this now. In these moments, I pulled out my sky blue plastic bag and began to pack my clothes. I was crying, I wanted out of this, when is this going to end, this is not fair, and where is my dad? I packed my bag with nowhere to go, I was just so tired. My brother saw my bag and said, do not leave! Where are you going? He told my mother about my bag, and he said you were going to make my sister run away. My mother said, "She's not going anywhere, I don't give a damn about her bags.

In the midst of the roller coaster of life experiencing joy, pain, up and downs, and creating memories with my mom. Deep down, over 25- years- ago, laid the painful memories that resurfaced during my writing season. Before I began to write this book, the Holy Spirit walked me through a season of forgiveness. I never felt like I hated my mother. We have always had a relationship but there was a topic I did not feel like I could talk to her about. I hated the addiction and I always felt like I did not deserve to go through it with her. This is why forgiveness is important because it is for you. My mother did the best she could do away with her addiction. The more I felt as though I did not deserve what I went through, it left an open door and I kept her and myself in bondage. It is okay for me to acknowledge my pain, but bondage leads to burdens. After I forgave her, we finally had the conversation I could not have with her due to guilt and shame, she had no idea how I felt and that I would switch roles with her. This conversation was difficult because the little girl, within me, did not want to feel rejected, muffled, or ignored tried to resurface. When I felt her, I pushed her out of the way to grab hold of my healing. I could feel the freedom— I had to walk through this for myself. Walking in freedom in this area has helped our relationship. I am aware when I try to make decisions for her and now I just simply shut up. It feels good and the burden is gone. We have as always had a great, supportive relationship, and I am glad that

**Now it makes sense, a lot of my suffering and
your suffering is because of our God given**

drugs did not steal our relationship— she is a great grandmother. My dad and I have conversations all the time and I can see a lot of myself in him, even the big head I have. True forgiveness is the road to healing. I did not have a father in the beginning years he missed ceremonies, violin concerts, band concerts, and high school graduation. However, my father was there for my graduation from graduate school and both of my parents walked me down the aisle on my wedding day. Reconciliation is beautiful! My God showed up redeemed the time.

Finishing Your Race of Life

Please understand that everything you have gone through happened to stop you from becoming the person you are destined to be. The enemy, yes, you have an enemy. He does not like you! His job is to stop you! He is committed to working overtime so that you never embrace your identity. That is why you have gone through so much. Do not give up hope! *Hebrews 12: 1-2* says "Therefore, since we are surrounded by such a huge crowd of witnesses to the life of faith, let us strip off every weight that slows us down, especially the sin that so easily trips us up. And let us run with endurance the race God has set before us. 2 We do this by keeping our eyes on Jesus, the champion who initiates and perfects our faith." I encourage you to push past all the pain, you are still breathing. The weight the Bible speaks of is our hurt, pain, disappointment, bitterness, and unforgiveness. I had a choice continue to conceal the past or trust the painful journey that has unlocked freedom.

The enemy did not win, there is always more. Your life is not over. Do not give up, fight for your life. Your future awaits you. Visualizing the end is better than your present; however, you have to get there. Life happens. Life is hard. What you put in it is what you will get out of it. After experiencing these situations in my childhood, my life continued to have hills and valleys. It does not benefit anyone to believe that he or she will not be faced with adversity in life. If you have been identified as a strong person, you may notice that, at times, it feels as if you cannot catch a break. Whatever you have told yourself in these moments, I want to challenge you to adopt a new language to your self-talk.

Do's

- First, accept that life will have high and low moments, and you will not be able to prepare for it all.

- Next, prophesy to yourself...I will live and not die! This will not overtake me! Recall the things that you have overcome in the past. Allow the victory in these moments to excite you, enlarge your hope, and launch your mind into strategies for the present.

- Finally, visualize yourself coming up; gradually, in every step, your hope and faith will increase as the situation decreases. I love scriptures because it breathes life, but you can adopt a song, scripture, affirmation, etc.

- Seek help. Mental counseling is potent to your mindset, depending on the issues you have endured.

Do not

- Faint

- Allow yourself to fall into depression without seeking help.

- Lose hope

- Give up

My Voice

New York had cold winters! It would snow, which I enjoyed making snow angels; however, the season did not work well with my skin. I had eczema in the worst place...my lips. Can you imagine? There was no hiding it at all. Every morning, my mother would put Vaseline on my face and kiss me. As we walked to school, I would walk behind her and wipe the Vaseline off because it made my face shiny. I remember wiping my face off with my shirt but it is hard to get the Vaseline off. I did not want a polished look. I did not want attention brought to my lips. At school, after breakfast, we would line up in the gym before reporting to class. A boy thought my shiny face was funny. He would look at me and say, "She looks like a grease monkey!" I did not respond; I just looked away, with hurtful feelings. Do you know how that made me feel? Of course, I was embarrassed, ashamed, and horrible, and I told my mother, but she continued to do it because mothers' know best. Deep inside, I did not want any attention brought to my lips. I made an inner vow not to put my children through the same thing when I grew up, and I kept my promise. I used lotion instead.

I did not feel accepted at all. The truth is no one's lips looked like mine. My thoughts were, ah man, I just wanted someone that could relate to me. I met a girl who had eczema all over her body, but her face and lips were clear. She wore long sleeves and long pants in the summertime. Eczema was dry, itchy, ashy, flaky, and hard to hide. One day, I took authority, and I shut my feelings down! I was fed up, tired of other kids' and adults' comments and opinions, hurting my feelings. More importantly, I had to accept the way my lips looked. I went home, locked the bathroom, stood on the toilet to see in the mirror, and said, "I don't care who likes me, God loves me just the way I am! God made me unique, and I love me! I cannot tell you where those words came from, but now that I am an adult; I recognize it as a God moment of empowering me. I said it, and I knew in my heart that He loved me…period!

God will take the pain of your past to shift you into your purpose.

As a middle school counselor, I talked to students who are working through identity issues. My thoughts were, it would be awesome if we spend more time building up each other, especially children. A sister and author of the book "Finally Set FREE" came in to co-teach a small group of girls who suffered from depression. Stacia Thorne beat cancer as a child, and overcame depression that followed. Stacia agreed to share her story with the students. The girls were handpicked due to the situations each of them were facing. We titled the group, "Imperfectly Enough." At the closeout session, we created mirrors for the young eighth-grade girls with words of affirmations. We created a mirror to speak to them when no one else would. We had one student who shared her feelings about herself during the group session. She sobbed as she explained how ugly she felt; the other girls hugged and encouraged her. They came together in unity. They told her how beautiful she. The small group only lasted 50- minutes and what she was going through was going on for 10- years. Her mirror was customized and said, "You are beautiful". Whenever she looked in that mirror, she did not have to say anything, but her eyes would lock in on the words you are beautiful. The goal of this was to cancel out the negative self-talk that was in her head. When she looks in the mirror, the mirror will let her know that she is beautiful. The atmosphere shifted when we presented the mirror to her. The tears rolled down her face as her friends embraced her. The goal of this group was fulfilled, teaching young girls to embrace themselves and support their friends.

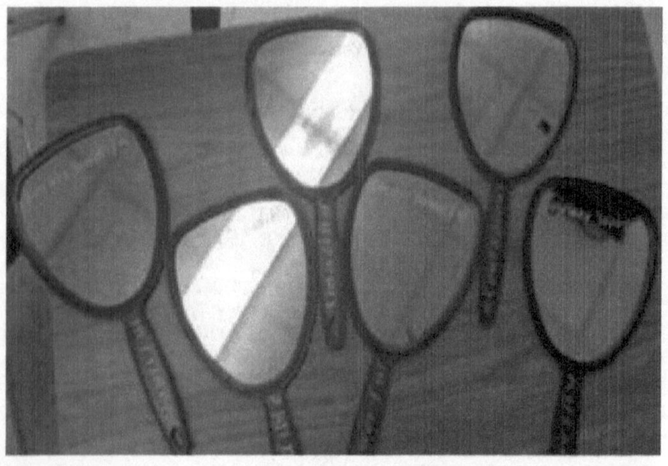

"God cares about our afflictions and adversities. Sometimes it seems like no one cares, but I will tell you, God does care."

Power of Words

Proverbs 18:21 confirms this by saying, "Death and life are in the power of the tongue, and those who love it will eat its fruits."

What I have learned is people pass judgment on you as you are going through life by speaking negative words over you and the situation. It does predict your future; however, if you receive their words, it can cripple you mentally. I heard some of the typical things like, "She will never be anything," but in my mind, it translated to, I can be anything I want to be. The power of self-talk works if you do the work. Sometimes, others felt as if they knew my story even though they were not living it. I want you to know that nobody can tell your story better than you can. I want you to know that a temporary situation does not define who you are or who you can become, and what the future holds for you. Allow every trying situation, every pitfall, every hurtful moment, and all the tears that you have shed to build up the ability for you to be resilient. All setbacks are a set up for a comeback. This is what I did! You may be wondering how you can say that; you do realize all of those situations are painful and traumatic. The truth of the matter is that you have to allow your circumstances to propel you forward. This is hope; hope is a choice! Words are powerful, and some terms carry a weight that will keep you in bondage. It was not until the age of 42 when I looked over my life that the word traumatic stood out.

I admitted my reality as the tears rolled down my face, and my heart skipped a beat. Quickly the Holy Spirit dried my tears and showed me that it was the past. It is in the rearview mirror, and none of it stopped me from becoming the person that I am. I was the first in my family to graduate from college with a Bachelor's degree and a Master's degree. I am the first homeowner. Now, I am using my test as my testimony to help others. Do not allow anyone's negative words to manifest in your life. God has given you the authority to speak into your life, to dream it, and to accomplish it.

Everything that you have experienced was only to make you who you are. I wish there was a magic wand that could take me away from what I was going through, but that was not an option. I had to make a choice. I could accept my mother's struggles as the way of life, or I can look around and find a positive person, someone that was winning at life, begin to dream and make my life different. My words gave me life, not what anyone else has said or thought about me.

Mindset Shift

Strategy	Reasoning	Action
Strategy 1 – "Face your Truth" What is going on? Do not suppress it!	It does not matter if it is your parent modeling the wrong behavior. You do not have to follow the same path. You have to	Hebrews 11:1 "Faith is the substance of things hoped for and the evidence of things not seen."
Do not ignore it! Do not take it lightly as if it will go away.	Choose your path, and it begins with the decision to stand for what is right.	
Strategy 2 Determining right from wrong.	I witness my mother have lots of fun, she would party, drink, and use drugs. Socially there is nothing wrong with this, right? However, some people do these things to get their mind off the	Choose the right path. The path that leads to hope, joy, and peace. The path that will bring you freedom. You will make mistakes, learn from them, and continue the

	pain of life and use it as a coping mechanism. That is a deception! Drugs and alcohol are temporarily numbing to an ongoing problem. After the temporary high goes away, the problem is still present.	course. If you get off the path, adjust yourself, get back in line, and keep going with no condemnation.
Strategy 3 *Mindset* Take your stand. Proverb 23:7 "As a man thinks in his heart so is he." No lie or negative word that has been spoken over you can dictate your future. *Do not allow your mind to adopt negativity into*	Refuse to believe what the enemy is showing you. If you do not like what you, see around you, feed yourself the opposite of what you see. This should encourage you. Embrace the fact that you do not deserve this style	Here is where you fight for yourself. Adopt a mantra You have more control over your life than anyone else does. It is okay the dream; this will allow you to have a vision for your life. Learn from the negative situations

your heart. Your past or current situation does not determine your future.	of life. Open your mind to the concept that your life can and will be better.	but focus on the positive
Strategy 4 Remain unmovable.	Adversity will come to its life. Do not conform to the situations but learn from the negative and allow the positive to push you forward. This is where wisdom comes from.	Feed yourself positive conversations. Find a mentor or someone that is living a life that you want. Talk to others that can inspire, influence, and empower you to finish your race.